fantastic fondue

fantastic fondue

for entertaining and special occasions

becky johnson

BARNES
&NOBLE
BOOKS
NEW YORK

This edition published by Barnes & Noble, Inc.,
by arrangement with Anness Publishing Limited

2003 Barnes & Noble Books

ISBN 0-7607- 5037-8

Printed in China

M 10 9 8 7 6 5 4 3 2 1

© Anness Publishing Limited 2003
Hermes House
88-89 Blackfriars Road
London SE1 8HA

Publisher: Joanna Lorenz
Managing Editor: Linda Fraser
Editorial Reader: Joy Wotton
Production Controller: Joanna King
Indexer: Hilary Bird
Designer: Paul Oakley at Blue Banana
Photography: Tim Auty
Props Styling: Helen Trent
Food Styling: Becky Johnson

Previously published as *Fondue*

Notes
Standard spoon and cup measures are level.
Large eggs are used unless otherwise stated.

Contents

Introduction

Fondues are hot – and that's not only their temperature. Their style is as funky as disco, as retro as a shag carpet and as kitsch as a lava lamp. Long associated with swinging parties and flower-power hippies, they now embody the spirit of modern cooking: fast, simple, flexible and, above all, social. So, if you have yet to jump on the fondue revival bandwagon, now is your chance.

Below: *Tabletop cooking is perfect for this fondue version of a Mongolian fire pot, where fresh vegetables and seafood are skewered on lemon grass sticks and then cooked in stock.*

Above: *Bread-crumbed fish slices are ideal for cooking in an oil fondue, as they take only a minute or two to cook.*

In this book, the term fondue is loosely defined as any liquid that is kept hot at the table so that each diner can dip morsels of food into it. Included are recipes with smooth, melted cheese sauces; flavorsome stocks for cooking tasty tidbits then drinking as a soup; and oil fondues where succulent meat, seafood and vegetables are crisply cooked before being dipped into mouth-watering sauces. Temptingly sweet fondues, with creamy or fruity sauces served with fruit or pastries, are also featured.

The recipes are all tried and tested and chosen from ideas gleaned from travels around the globe. They usually require some advance preparation, but this has been kept to a minimum. The real joy of the fondue becomes apparent once the diners are seated and everyone is able to participate in the cooking process. This takes some of the pressure away from the host and allows the diners to become involved in the shared, relaxed and fun experience that is the fondue.

The recipes begin with an old favorite: the creamy, traditional Swiss cheese fondue. Later in the book, other cuisines from around the world are represented: roasted tomato and mascarpone fondue with eggplant fritters from Italy, spiced Moroccan meatballs with harissa dip from North Africa and the aromatic, Thai-inspired tom yam.

Dessert fondues include a heavenly chocolate fondue with meltingly sweet poached pears and ice cream for dipping. If you prefer an exotic and fruity dessert, banana fritters with papaya cream or blackberry fondue with figs and frangipane pastries are guaranteed to fire up even the most jaded of palates.

Hopefully the ideas in this book will inspire you to invite friends and family to take part in this informal way of eating. So bring out the burners and the long forks and enjoy a return to the relaxed sociable dining, if not the heady, flower-power days, of the 1970s.

Above: *Fresh blackberry puree is just one of the many sweet fondues, which range from smooth, creamy custard and rich chocolate sauce to papaya cream with deep-fried fritters for dipping.*

Above: *Big garlicky croutons make a change from the cubes of bread that are traditionally dipped into a Swiss cheese fondue.*

Equipment

It is not necessary to go out and purchase a fondue set if you want to host a fondue party, but you will need a few essentials.

Heat source
A small night light or candle is the simplest form of heat source that you could use, and this is perfectly sufficient for a chocolate fondue. However, it does not produce enough heat for either oil or stock fondues. For these you will need to use a Sterno burner, or a special stainless steel burner, of which there are two types. One contains a sponge onto which liquid alcohol fuel is poured, and then ignited. The other comprises a small foil tray of gel-based fuel that simply slides into the burner and is discarded when used. A lid covers the burner, which can be adjusted to regulate the heat. Burners also have the advantage of being spill-proof so that any accidents are avoided. Electric fondue sets are available, which help to keep oil fondues up to temperature, but they do detract from the romance of a real flame.

Fire pots
The Mongolian fire pot incorporates a large, usually aluminum pot with a central funnel above a rack onto which burning coals or night-lights are placed to heat the stock.

Above: Liquid alcohol fuel burners (left) and gel burners (top right) will create enough heat to cook both oil and stock fondues. Tiny night-light candles (bottom right) are only suitable for keeping sauces warm, but they are less likely to scorch delicate sauces such as cheese or chocolate.

Right: The traditional aluminum Mongolian fire pot is ideal for cooking stock-based fondues, but there's no need to go out and buy one specially as you can use a large pan, small wok or flameproof casserole instead.

Above: *Fondue pots may have one or two handles. Pots with two handles are safer for oil and stock fondues.*

Pot holders or racks

Fondue stands comprise a rack, on which the pan or fondue pot is supported, and a base on which the burner or night-light sits.

Fondue pots

It is not necessary to use a special fondue pot. Any pan, flameproof casserole or pot can sit on the rack as long as it is secure. Stainless steel is best for oil fondues, and any heavy-based pot for delicate cheese or sauce fondues.

Right: *Dinner forks are fine for dipping foods into sauce fondues, but use special long-handled forks or skewers for cooking in stock or oil.*

Fondue sets

Inexpensive fondue sets are available that incorporate a pot, stand, forks and a burner. Cheaper sets with just a rack and burner can also be bought, as can individual pots and pans, forks and skewers.

Cutlery

Dinner forks can be used for dipping food into a fondue. However, when cooking food in the fondue, forks with handles are needed, as the metal of a fork or skewer will get dangerously hot when left in the fondue. Small wire baskets can be used to fish out food that has been deep-fried or cooked in stock. Chopsticks or small wooden tongs are the authentic equipment for cooking sukiyaki and tempura.

Above: *Some fondue sets include a splash guard to protect diners' hands and support the forks while cooking.*

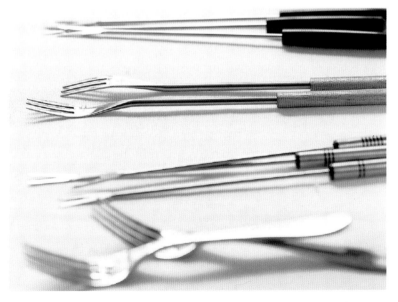

Techniques
and Guidelines

Fondues work best with small quantities, so don't invite too many guests – four or six people is about right. Check whether your fondue pot can be used on the stove, and if not, prepare the fondue in a small pan and then transfer to the fondue pot. Ask diners to stir sauce fondues using a figure-eight motion with their dipping food, to keep the fondue creamy.

Cheese fondues

To add flavor, rub the inside of the fondue pot with the cut side of a garlic clove.

Grate or crumble cheese to help it melt quickly, and heat it gently, as it burns easily.

The finished fondue should have a smooth and creamy consistency. If this is not the case, add a squeeze of lemon juice to help it bind together.

Below: *When dipping, stir the sauce in a figure eight to keep it smooth.*

Stock fondues

Use a well-flavored vegetable or chicken stock and don't overfill the pan – it should be no more than two-thirds full. Add noodles or pasta to the stock, if you like, then serve as a soup once the food dippers have all been cooked.

Oil fondues

Use a cook's thermometer to check the oil temperature – it should be 375°F.

Alternately, test the temperature by dropping a cube of day-old bread into the hot oil; it should brown in 30–60 seconds. If you transfer the oil from a pan to the fondue pot, place the fondue pot in the sink while you pour. Ensure that the pot is no more than two-thirds full.

Once the oil has been transferred to the table, adjust the burner to its highest setting (with all the air holes fully open). Don't cook too much food at one time, as this will cool the oil and may cause it to foam up and overflow. You may need to reheat the oil on the stove if the temperature drops too much.

Sweet fondues

Custards, fruit purees and chocolate sauces can be cooked ahead of time and chilled until ready to reheat and serve. Cook custards gently, as they may curdle and become grainy if overheated. If this should happen, plunge the base of the pan into a bowl of cold water to cool it quickly and add a little cold milk or cream, whisking rapidly.

Ensure that fruit sauces are thick enough to coat the food for dipping – if not, thicken with a little blended cornstarch.

When melting chocolate, don't allow the bowl to get too hot, or the chocolate may overheat and "seize". Add liquids such as cream, coffee or liqueur before melting, and don't stir until the chocolate has melted completely.

Above: A night-light candle is the best option for reheating delicate fondues, such as custard or chocolate, that scorch easily if overheated.

Ingredients

The beauty of fondues is their simplicity: only a few ingredients are required to create an appealing and satisfying meal, but it is the imaginative combination of tastes that gives fondues their magic.

Above: Soft cheeses such as goat cheese are usually melted in milk rather than lemon juice or alcohol.

Cheese

The classic cheese fondues use mild-flavored cheeses from Switzerland, such as Emmenthal, Gruyère and Appenzeller, which have an elastic texture when melted. They need to be cooked with acidic wines, liqueurs or lemon juice to help produce a smooth fondue. Other suitable cheeses include Beaufort, mozzarella, Edam, Fontina and Cheddar; try them for their subtle differences of taste and texture.

For the lighter, less alcoholic soft-cheese fondues, choose strong to mild-flavored goat cheeses or very mild but tangy soft cheeses

Above: Hard cheeses should be teamed with dry, acidic wines, such as Zinfandel or Swiss Chasselas.

such as herb or pepper-flavored cream cheese, ricotta or mascarpone. The strong tastes of blue cheeses are also excellent, from the creamy Dolcelatte, Bleu d'Auvergne and Gorgonzola to the more pungent and crumblier Stilton. These cheeses are melted in milk instead of alcohol or lemon juice.

Alcohol

Use a dry and acidic wine with hard cheeses. A good choice is Swiss Chasselas or any full-flavored, dry white wine.

For a fruity flavor try hard cider, or, if you are using a good, sharp, British hard cheese, a real-ale beer makes a full-flavored fondue.

Right: Firm cheeses such as Gruyère and Emmenthal need to be cooked with wine, liqueur or lemon juice.

Liqueurs add flavor and ensure a smooth cheese fondue – Kirsch is a favorite. Enhance a chocolate fondue with the orange flavor of Cointreau or Grand Marnier, or use coffee Kahlúa or almond-flavored Disaronno Amaretto. Fruit liqueurs will transform fruit-puree fondues, adding a rich flavor.

Oil

Light-colored and mild-flavored oils, which can be heated to high temperatures without smoking, are best for oil fondues. Choose from vegetable, corn, sunflower, peanut or soya oils. Olive, sesame and nut oils are too strongly flavored to be suitable and are inclined to burn at high temperatures. If you enjoy the flavor of these oils, add one or two spoonfuls to one of the milder oils.

Below: *Choose mild-flavored oils such as vegetable and sunflower for oil fondues.*

Chocolate

The most expensive chocolates are usually the best for a fondue, as they contain a larger proportion of cocoa solids, sometimes as much as 90 percent compared to 17 percent in a cheaper variety. These good-quality dark chocolates are also known as bitter chocolate; they contain very little cream or vegetable fat and no sugar. You will need to use less than the cheaper alternatives to achieve a good taste. Try organic cooking chocolate or Valrhona chocolate. Even when cream and sugar are added to a chocolate fondue, the rich flavor of the chocolate will remain. For a sweeter and milder fondue use good quality milk or white chocolate. Don't use chocolate cake icing for a fondue – the flavor simply isn't good enough.

Whatever the chocolate you choose, melt it carefully in a bowl over a pan of hot, but not boiling, water and don't allow it to overheat.

Above: *Good quality, strongly flavored chocolate with a high proportion of cocoa solids is best for fondues.*

Simple Dippers

A selection of natural and ready-made foods make ideal dippers for a fondue, with little or no preparation. These dippers can often be hand-held, but some may need to be speared onto long-handled fondue forks.

Above and right: Bread sticks make great dippers, as do gherkins, tortilla chips and olives.

Bread, potato chips and crackers

Choose bread with different textures: French sticks, bagels, sourdough and soda breads, seeded breads, such as poppy-seed-crusted breads, and nut breads. Also try Italian breads, such as sun-dried tomato, onion or olive focaccia and ciabatta. If you can, match the

Right: Croutons make tasty bitesize dippers, but slices of fresh bread are equally good.

bread to the cheese: a Dolcelatte fondue will pair perfectly with sun-dried tomato bread and olive focaccia, for example. The bread can be cubed or sliced and eaten fresh, grilled, toasted or fried in a little butter and oil until crisp.

Potato chips and crackers also make simple dippers for cheese fondues. Try corn chips, bread sticks – plain or wrapped in prosciutto – or cheese straws. Make sure that they are large enough to be hand-held while dipped into the fondue, and that they will not disintegrate once laden with the sauce.

For sweet fondues, cubes or slices of sweet breads such as croissants and brioche make good dippers.

Fruit

Some fruits, such as grapes and apples, are suitable for dipping into savory as well as sweet fondues. Take advantage of fruits in season for sweet fondues: strawberries, cherries, plums, peaches, apricots and nectarines are all suitable, as well as exotic fruits such as figs, pineapple, papayas, mangoes, star fruit and lychees. Fruits available all year, such as bananas and the citrus fruits, also dip well. Underripe fruit can be lightly poached in sugar syrup, fruit juice or a fruity wine; this works especially well for pears.

Cakes, pastries and cookies

Slices of dense-textured cake, and pastries or cookies make excellent dippers for sweet fondues. Try pound cake, meringues, Danish pastries, biscotti, or chocolate-chip cookies – whatever you fancy.

Vegetables

Fresh, raw vegetable dippers, prepared as crudités, add a light crunch to a cheese fondue. Choose from pink radishes, baby carrots, baby corn, sugar snap peas or snow peas, red, orange and yellow bell peppers, young celery, Belgian endive, cucumber and fennel. Some vegetables, such as asparagus spears, cauliflower or broccoli florets, baby leeks and green beans, are best lightly blanched in salted boiling water until they are lightly cooked, but still retain their crunch.

Above: Crunchy, fresh vegetables perfectly complement a creamy cheese fondue, while biscotti, small fruits and cakes (top left) are wonderful with sweet fondues.

Left: For chocolate fondues, small cubes of firm-textured cakes go well with a selection of exotic fruits.

Cheese
fondues

Creamy sauces made from melted cheese make delectable dips for all kinds of foods. Try rich and flavorful Dolcelatte fonduta, mild roasted tomato and mascarpone fondue or goat cheese fondue.

INGREDIENTS

Serves 4–6

2 French batons or 1 baguette

1–2 garlic cloves, halved

1 small head broccoli, divided
    into florets

1 small head cauliflower, divided
    into florets

7 ounces snow peas or green
    beans, trimmed

4 ounces baby carrots, trimmed,
    or 2 medium carrots, cut into
    long wedges

8 fluid ounces/1 cup dry
    white wine

4 ounces/1 cup grated
    Gruyère cheese

9 ounces/2 1/4 cups grated
    Emmenthal cheese

1 tablespoon cornstarch

2 tablespoons Kirsch

freshly grated nutmeg

salt and ground black pepper

For the dressing

2 tablespoons extra virgin
    olive oil

rind and juice of 2 lemons

1 ounce/1/2 cup chopped
    fresh parsley

1 ounce/1/2 cup chopped
    fresh mint

1 red chile, seeded and
    finely chopped

This classic, richly flavored fondue is traditionally served with cubes of bread, but here it's updated with herbed vegetable dippers and garlic toast.

Swiss Cheese
Fondue with Warm, Herbed Vegetables and Garlic Croutons

Cut the French batons or baguette on the diagonal into 1/2-inch slices, then toast on both sides. Rub one side of each toasted slice with the cut side of a garlic clove, if you like, and transfer to a serving platter.

Blanch all the vegetables for two minutes in a large pan of salted boiling water, then place them in a large bowl. While they are hot, add all the dressing ingredients, season, and toss together.

Rub the inside of the fondue pot with the cut side of a garlic clove. Pour in the wine and heat gently on the stove. Gradually add the grated cheeses, stirring constantly until melted. Mix the cornstarch with the Kirsch and add, then stir until thickened.

Season with salt, pepper and grated nutmeg to taste. When the fondue is hot and smooth, but not boiling, transfer to a burner at the table.

Each diner dips the vegetables and toasted bread into the fondue.

Serves 6

8 ounces/1 cup strained
    plain yogurt
$^1/_4$ pint/$^2/_3$ cup milk
1 pound feta cheese, crumbled
1 tablespoon cornstarch
1$^1/_4$ pounds watermelon, cut
    into 6 wedges
salt and ground black pepper
warmed pitta bread, Greek
    marinated olives and salad,
    to serve

For the spicy sardines

3 tablespoons olive oil
2 shallots, finely chopped
3 garlic cloves, crushed
1 red chile, seeded and
    finely chopped
small bunch cilantro or Italian
    parsley, finely chopped
12 fresh sardines, cleaned and
    backbones removed
juice of 1 lemon

Conjure up thoughts of relaxing holidays on hot, sunny Greek islands with this mezze-inspired dish. Salty olives, chile-spiced sardines and fresh watermelon make perfect partners for this creamy yogurt and feta fondue.

Feta Fondue with Spicy Sardines and Watermelon

Soak 12 toothpicks in cold water for 30 minutes. Prepare the spicy sardines. Heat 1 tablespoon of the oil in a frying pan and add the shallots and garlic. Cook for a few minutes, then add the chile and cilantro or parsley. Spread the onion mixture over the flesh-side of the sardines, roll them up from the head to the tail and secure with a toothpick.

Gently heat the yogurt and milk together until hot but not boiling, then add the cheese and stir until smooth. Blend the cornstarch with 2 tablespoons of water and stir into the cheese mixture. Season. Cook gently until thickened, then transfer to a fondue pot and place on a burner at the table.

To cook the sardines, heat the remaining olive oil in a frying pan and fry the sardines for 3–4 minutes. Add the lemon juice and transfer to a serving platter. Diners dip the sardines into the fondue. Serve the fondue with chunky watermelon wedges, warm pitta bread, olives and salad.

INGREDIENTS

Serves 4–6

8 fluid ounces/1 cup milk

6 thyme sprigs, woody stems removed, chopped, plus extra thyme leaves for garnishing

7 ounces/scant 1 cup light cream cheese

4 ounces/1/2 cup young, soft goat cheese

1 tablespoon cornstarch

salt and ground black pepper

For the potatoes

1 pound fatty bacon strips

2 1/4 pounds small new potatoes, scrubbed

24 small bay leaves

VARIATIONS

• Use fresh parsley instead of thyme, if you prefer.

• Try Italian pancetta instead of the bacon and wrap each potato with one or two fresh basil leaves in place of the bay.

Bay-scented baby potatoes wrapped with thin strips of bacon and then dipped into tangy melting goat cheese make a sublime mouthful.

Goat Cheese and Thyme Fondue with Crispy Bacon Baked Potatoes

First, prepare the potatoes. Preheat the oven to 400°F/Gas 6. Stretch each bacon strip with the back of a knife, then slice in half across the middle. Wrap each of the potatoes and a bay leaf in a piece of bacon and then place them join side down in a baking tray. Season with pepper and bake for 30–35 minutes, or until the potatoes are tender and the bacon is crisp.

Meanwhile, heat all but 2 tablespoons of the milk with the thyme until hot but not boiling. Add the cream cheese and the goat cheese, then beat or whisk the mixture until it is smooth.

Blend the cornstarch to a paste with the remaining milk, then add to the fondue and stir until thick. Season with salt and pepper, then transfer to a fondue pot, scatter a little extra thyme on top of the fondue mixture and place on a burner at the table.

Serve the hot, bacon-wrapped potatoes for dipping into the fondue. You can either eat the crisp bay leaves, or remove them.

INGREDIENTS

Serves 4

3/4 pint/scant 2 cups milk

7 ounces Dolcelatte cheese, diced

4 ounces/1 cup grated mozzarella cheese

1 tablespoon cornstarch

4 tablespoons dry white wine

salt and ground black pepper

For the rosemary skewers

12 woody rosemary stems, about 6 inches long

12 slices prosciutto, sliced in half lengthwise

14 ounces walnut bread loaf, cut into large cubes

12 ready-to-eat prunes, pitted

2 zucchini, halved lengthwise and cut into 1/2-inch slices

1 ounce/2 tablespoons butter

2 tablespoons olive oil

1 garlic clove, crushed

VARIATIONS

The rosemary sticks could be threaded with a variety of quick-cooking foods, from pieces of sausage to firm fish such as salmon or cod, and vegetables, such as mushrooms or cherry tomatoes.

Fonduta is the Italian version of the fondue, and it is usually made from mixtures of Fontina, Provolone or Gorgonzola cheeses. For this recipe, creamy Dolcelatte cheese is mixed with the lighter mozzarella.

Dolcelatte Fonduta
with Rosemary Skewers

Remove all but the top leaves from the rosemary stems and soak them in cold water for 30 minutes. Gently heat the milk on the stove in a fondue pot, then add the cheeses and stir until smooth. Season well.

Blend the cornstarch with the wine, add to the cheese mixture and stir until thickened.

Meanwhile, prepare the rosemary skewers. Take a soaked rosemary skewer and thread on one end of a piece of prosciutto. Add a bread

cube, a prune and one or two slices of zucchini, interleaving the proscuitto between the ingredients, so that the prosciutto is speared several times. Repeat with the other rosemary sticks.

Heat the butter with the oil in a large frying pan and gently fry the garlic for a few minutes. Add the skewers to the frying pan and cook for a minute on each side until hot and golden brown.

Place the fondue pot on a burner at the table. Diners remove the vegetables from the skewers and use fondue forks to dip the vegetables into the hot fondue.

INGREDIENTS

Serves 4–6

*2¹/4 pounds very ripe tomatoes,
  on the vine*
*3 tablespoons olive oil, plus
  extra for shallow frying*
*1 large onion,
  finely chopped*
2 garlic cloves, crushed
*2 tablespoons Worcestershire
  sauce*
1 teaspoon brown sugar
*9 ounces/generous 1 cup
  mascarpone cheese*
*small bunch basil or Italian
  parsley, torn or chopped*
salt and ground black pepper

For the fritters

*18 baby eggplants, sliced in half
  lengthwise, or 2 medium
  eggplants, each cut into
  ¹/2-inch thick slices
  then halved to make
  half-moon shapes*
6³/4-ounce jar pesto
*7 ounces/scant 1 cup polenta
  valsugana, or pre-cooked
  maize meal*

VARIATION

*For a change, replace the plain
pesto with red bell pepper
pesto, a fresh cilantro pesto,
olive paste or, for a fiery touch,
add a little harissa.*

A piquant and creamy tomato sauce is heavenly for dipping crisp polenta and pesto eggplant fritters. Use very ripe tomatoes for the best flavor.

Roasted Tomato and Mascarpone Fondue with Eggplant Fritters

Preheat the oven to 400°F/Gas 6. Place the tomatoes in a roasting pan, season with salt and pepper and drizzle over 2 tablespoons of the oil. Roast for 20 minutes.

Meanwhile, heat the remaining oil in a large frying pan and sauté the onion and garlic over a low heat for about 10 minutes, or until softened, but not browned. Remove the skins from the roasted tomatoes, then add to the pan with the Worcestershire sauce, sugar and a little more seasoning, and cook for 15–20 minutes, breaking up the tomatoes with a wooden spoon.

To make the fritters, spread the cut sides of the eggplants with a little pesto. Put the polenta on a plate and press the pesto-coated eggplants into it. Heat the oil for frying in a large frying pan and fry the eggplants in batches for 3–4 minutes on each side.

Stir the mascarpone and basil or parsley into the tomato sauce. Transfer to a fondue pot and place on a burner at the table. Serve with the fritters for dipping.

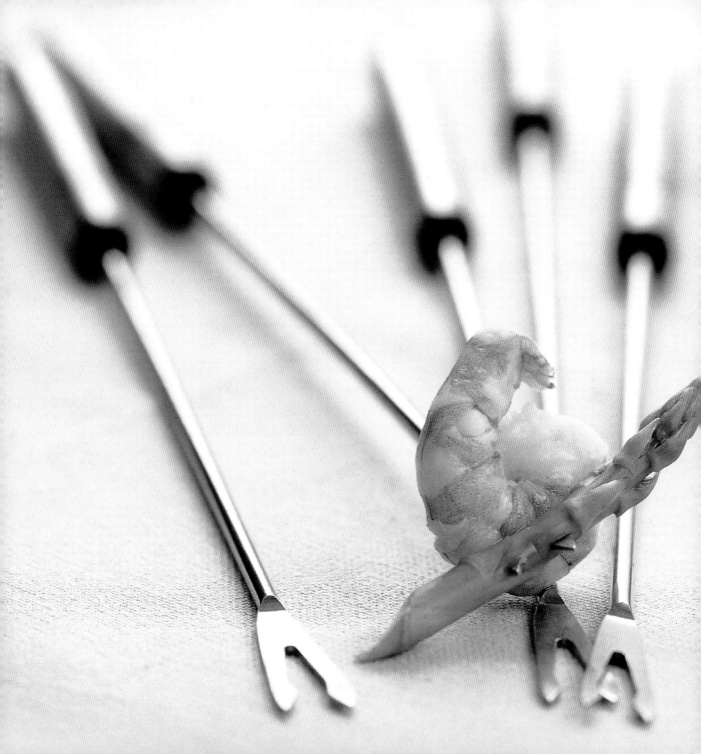

Stock
fondues

In these unusual fondues, guests cook bitesize portions of fish, small shellfish, morsels of meat, vegetables and tofu and even stuffed pasta in flavorsome, simmering stocks at the table.

INGREDIENTS

Serves 4–6

8–12 whole raw jumbo shrimp,
    peeled and de-veined, with tails on

2 skinless salmon or tuna fillets,
    about 5 ounces each

6 sachets instant miso soup mixed
    with 3 pints/7 1/2 cups water or
    the same quantity of fish, chicken
    or vegetable stock

handful of cilantro leaves

2–3 scallions, sliced

small bunch watercress, arugula or
    young mizuma greens

2 ounces enoki mushrooms

7 ounces fine egg noodles

8–12 lemon grass stalks or
    wooden skewers

soy sauce and wasabi paste or
    horseradish sauce, to serve

For the marinade

rind and juice of 2 limes

2 tablespoons soy sauce

1-inch piece ginger root, peeled and
    finely chopped

2 garlic cloves, finely chopped

1 tablespoon clear honey

1 red chile, seeded and chopped

COOK'S TIP

*To make them easier to eat,
snip the noodles into short
lengths using a pair of scissors.*

In this easy-to-prepare fondue, pretty pink shrimp tails and cubes of fish are marinated with garlic, ginger and chile, then skewered with fragrant lemon grass stalks before being cooked at the table in a flavorful stock.

Mongolian Fire Pot

Wash the shrimp, pat dry and place in a deep serving bowl. Cut the salmon or tuna fillets into 1-inch cubes and add to the shrimp.

Mix all the marinade ingredients together and add to the bowl of seafood. Toss gently to coat, then cover and leave the seafood to marinate in the refrigerator for a minimum of 10 minutes, or 2 hours if possible.

Pour the stock into a pan, add the cilantro and scallions and bring to the boil. Transfer to a fondue pot and place on a burner at the table or pour the stock into a fire pot at the table and keep hot.

Arrange the salad leaves and mushrooms on serving plates, and put the soy sauce and wasabi or horseradish into small bowls. Add the noodles to the stock at the table and leave to cook.

Invite each diner to spear a cube of fish or a shrimp onto a lemon grass stalk or skewer with a salad leaf and a mushroom. This is then submerged in the stock for 1 minute, or until the fish or shrimp is cooked, then dipped into the soy sauce and wasabi or horseradish. When the fish and vegetables are all eaten, divide the remaining stock and noodles among soup bowls to eat.

INGREDIENTS

Serves 4–6

1 pound beef tenderloin
9 ounces tofu, cut into
  1/2-inch cubes
7 ounces sugar snap peas or
  green beans sliced diagonally
  in half
1 bunch purple scallions, sliced
  diagonally into 1-inch pieces
juice of 1 lime
small bunch of cilantro, chopped
lime wedges and boiled jasmine
  and wild rice, to serve

For the marinade

1-inch piece fresh
  ginger root, peeled and
  finely chopped
1 garlic clove, crushed
1 tablespoon wholegrain
  mustard
4 tablespoons soy sauce
1 tablespoon sesame oil

For the warishita stock

2 tablespoons brown sugar
3 tablespoons mirin or
  sweet sherry
3 1/2 fluid ounces/scant 1/2 cup
  soy sauce
3 1/2 fluid ounces/scant 1/2 cup
  vegetable stock

Thin slices of tender, marinated beef, tofu and vegetables are fried and then simmered in a sweet stock at the table in this Japanese dish. They are then dipped in a delicious ginger and mustard marinade before they are eaten.

Sukiyaki

Place the beef tenderloin between two pieces of parchment paper and beat out with a meat bat or rolling pin until thin. Cut into 1-inch wide, bitesize strips.

Place all the marinade ingredients in a large dish, add the beef and tofu and toss together until well coated. Set aside. Mix the warishita stock ingredients together in a bowl or pitcher.

Heat a small wok or frying pan until very hot, then transfer to a burner at the table. Add the marinated beef and tofu to the hot wok and cook for a few seconds on each side, turning with tongs or long chopsticks. Add the warishita stock and the vegetables to the wok or pan and cook for a few minutes, or until tender, then add the lime juice and cilantro. Spoon the marinade into individual dipping saucers.

Diners help themselves from the wok with their chopsticks and eat the sukiyaki dipped in the marinade and served with lime wedges and bowls of jasmine and wild rice.

VARIATION
Sukiyaki can also be made using venison or tuna steaks in place of the fillet steak.

INGREDIENTS

Serves 4–6

7 ounces raw shrimp, peeled
    and de-veined
12 ounces cod fillet, or other firm
    white fish, skin removed
1 bunch scallions, chopped
2 kaffir lime leaves,
    finely chopped
1 lemon grass stalk,
    finely chopped
1 tablespoon soy sauce
2 tablespoons cornstarch
2 1/2 pints/6 1/4 cups instant miso
    soup or chicken stock
7 ounces cellophane noodles,
    soaked in cold water
small bunch cilantro, chopped,
    to garnish

For the marinated baby corn

1 red chile, seeded and
    finely chopped
1/2-inch ginger root, peeled
    and grated
1 teaspoon honey
1 teaspoon rice vinegar
1 teaspoon sesame oil
1 tablespoon chopped
    fresh cilantro
4 1/2 ounces baby corn

This unique Thai dish combines hot, sour, savory and sweet flavors. Small shrimp balls scented with lemon grass and kaffir lime leaves are cooked in an aromatic stock and eaten with sweet, crunchy, marinated baby corn.

Tom Yam Soup

Rinse the shrimp and pat dry. Remove any bones from the white fish. Place the shrimp, fish, scallions, kaffir lime leaves, lemon grass and soy sauce in a food processor or blender and blend to a rough paste. Roll into cherry-tomato-size balls, dust lightly with cornstarch, then place in a single layer on a serving platter and chill until required.

To make the marinated baby corn, mix the chile, ginger, honey, rice vinegar, oil and chopped cilantro in a serving bowl, add the baby corn and leave to marinate for 1–2 hours.

Bring the stock to the boil in a fondue pot. Snip the noodles into short lengths with scissors, and add to the stock with the cilantro. Transfer to a burner at the table.

Diners help themselves to the shrimp balls, dropping them into the hot stock for a minute or so, until pink and cooked through. Serve with the marinated baby corn, skewering these onto toothpicks to make them easy to hold.

When all the shrimp balls are cooked and eaten, ladle the stock with the noodles into individual warmed soup bowls to eat.

INGREDIENTS

Serves 4

1 chicken, about 5 pounds
1 parsley sprig
1 tablespoon black peppercorns
1 bay leaf
11 ounces baby carrots
6 ounces baby leeks
1 ounce/2 tablespoons butter
1 tablespoon olive oil
11 ounces shallots, halved
   if large
7 fluid ounces/scant 1 cup dry
   white wine
1³/4 pounds baby new potatoes
4 fluid ounces/¹/2 cup
   heavy cream
salt and ground black pepper
small bunch parsley or tarragon,
   chopped, to garnish

In France, a pot au feu traditionally contains beef simmered in a rich stock, although chicken is also used. In this recipe, a lovely wine and herb-scented stock contains tender morsels of chicken and spring vegetables.

Chicken Pot au Feu

Joint the chicken into eight pieces and place the carcass in a large stockpot. Add the parsley sprig, peppercorns, bay leaf and the trimmings from the carrots and leeks. Cover with cold water and bring to the boil. Simmer for 45 minutes, then strain. Meanwhile, melt the butter with the olive oil in a frying pan, then add the chicken pieces, season, and brown all over. Lift out the chicken pieces onto a plate and add the shallots to the pan. Cook over a low heat for 20 minutes, stirring occasionally, until softened, but not browned.

Return the chicken to the pan and add the wine. Scrape up any juices from the bottom of the pan with a wooden spoon, then add the carrots, leeks and potatoes with enough of the stock to just cover. Bring to the boil, then cover and simmer for 20 minutes. Stir in the cream.

Transfer to a fondue pot and place on a burner at the table. Diners help themselves, sprinkling over the herbs.

COOK'S TIPS

• Any leftover stock can be kept in the refrigerator and used in other recipes.
• You could use large potatoes, but they will need to be par-boiled first so that they will cook in 10–15 minutes in the pot with the other ingredients.

INGREDIENTS

Serves 4–6

1 1/2 pounds butternut squash

4 ounces/1 1/3 cups freshly
  grated Parmesan cheese

1 bunch parsley, finely chopped

2 ounces/1/2 cup pine
  nuts, toasted

1 1/4 pounds fresh lasagne
  sheets

1 egg, beaten

1 1/2 pints/3 3/4 cups fresh
  chicken stock

salt and ground black pepper

For the sauce

2 ounces/1/3 cup walnut pieces

5 ready-to-eat dried apricots,
  roughly chopped

2 slices whole-wheat bread

9 ounces/generous 1 cup
  ricotta cheese

2 1/2 fluid ounces/1/3 cup milk

COOK'S TIP

To toast pine nuts, spread them
in a broiling pan and heat
under a hot broiler for
2 minutes. Stir or shake the pan
frequently to prevent them from
burning. Alternately, put them in
a pan and dry-fry them briefly,
until they turn golden in color
and give off a wonderful aroma.

The perfect Italian-inspired recipe for cooking at the table – little ravioli pillows cooked in a tasty broth and served with a superb creamy nut sauce.

Walnut Sauce
with Butternut Squash Ravioli

Preheat the oven to 400°F/Gas 6. Bake the squash on a baking tray for 45 minutes.

Cut the baked squash in half lengthwise, remove the seeds and scoop out the flesh. Put the flesh into a food processor with the grated Parmesan cheese, half the parsley, the pine nuts and seasoning, and blend to a rough puree.

Using a 2½-inch fluted cookie cutter, cut out two round pieces from each lasagne sheet. Put 1 teaspoon of the squash mixture into the center of half of the round pieces, then brush the edges of each one with a little beaten egg. Place a second round piece on top of each one, then pinch together the edges to make ravioli. Transfer to a serving platter.

To make the sauce, place the walnuts, apricots, bread and remaining parsley in a food processor or blender and process to fairly fine crumbs. Add the ricotta cheese and pulse to mix. Spoon into

a pan, add the milk, then heat gently, stirring constantly until smooth. Pour the sauce into a warmed serving pitcher.

Heat the stock in a fondue pot to boiling point, and then place on a burner at the table.

Invite diners to drop their own ravioli into the stock for 2–3 minutes. When cooked, fish them out with wire baskets, long-handled forks or tongs, and eat with the warm walnut sauce.

Oil
fondues

In these fondues, delicious tidbits, quickly fried at the table, are served with flavorful sauces for dipping. Try crab cakes with Thai relish, crisp fish slices with guacamole or Japanese tempura.

INGREDIENTS

Serves 4–6

1 pound sole or pink
    trout fillets
4 ounces/1 cup all-purpose flour
2 teaspoons chili powder
2 eggs, beaten
7 ounces/3½ cups fresh
    bread crumbs
oil, for deep-frying
salt and ground black pepper
4–6 soft wheat tortillas, cut
    into wedges
lime wedges, to serve

For the guacamole

4 large ripe avocados
juice and thinly pared and
    shredded rind of 2 limes
1 garlic clove, crushed
7 fluid ounces/scant 1 cup
    crème fraîche or sour cream
2 scallions, finely chopped

COOK'S TIP

*A Mexican trick of pushing the
avocado pit back into the
center of the prepared
guacamole and then covering
it tightly with plastic wrap
prevents the guacamole from
discoloring. Remove the stone
before serving.*

**Small pieces of sole or trout are given
a spicy coating, with a hint of chili,
and crisply fried at the table. They are
served with an extra-creamy version of
guacamole in this tasty combination of
French and Mexican cuisine.**

Chili-crusted Fish
with Guacamole and Tortillas

Cut the fish fillets on the diagonal into pieces about ¼-inch thick and 2½ inches long. Mix the flour
with the chili powder and salt on a plate. Put the eggs into a shallow bowl. Dip the fish first in the
chili flour, then the egg and finally the bread crumbs. Place on a serving platter and chill.

To make the guacamole, cut the avocados in half and remove the pits, then scoop out the flesh
and mash with the lime juice, garlic, crème fraîche and scallions. Season with salt and pepper. Put
into a serving bowl, garnish with the lime shreds, and chill until ready to serve.

Heat the oil in a wok or
pan to 375°F, or test by
dropping a cube of day-old
bread into the hot oil; it
should brown in 30–60
seconds. Place the wok or pan
on a burner at the table.

Invite each diner to drop
the fish slices into the hot oil
for 2 minutes, or until golden.
Deep-fry the tortilla pieces
for a few seconds. Remove
with tongs. Eat with the
guacamole accompanied by
lime wedges for squeezing.

INGREDIENTS

Serves 4–6

2 teaspoons chili flakes
1 tablespoon cumin seeds
1/2-inch piece of cinnamon stick
1 teaspoon mustard seeds
1 teaspoon ground turmeric
14 ounce can chickpeas, drained
14 ounces ground meat
1 large onion, finely chopped
2 large garlic cloves, crushed
1 egg
1 tablespoon Worcestershire
    sauce
2 tablespoons tomato paste
small bunch parsley, chopped
salt and ground black pepper
oil, for deep-frying

For the harissa dip

8 ounces/1 cup thick strained
    plain yogurt
1 1/2 tablespoons rose water
2 teaspoons harissa

COOK'S TIPS

• *Lamb, beef or chicken can be*
used for the meatballs.
• *If you'd prefer to make them*
vegetarian, use vegetarian
mince and omit the
Worcestershire sauce.

Harissa is a hot and spicy chili sauce, which makes a delicious dip when mixed with rose water and yogurt. It is the perfect accompaniment for these dainty and spicy meatballs, which are cooked at the table in a few minutes.

Spiced Moroccan
Meatballs with Harissa Dip

Grind the chili, cumin, cinnamon, mustard seeds and turmeric together in a mortar and pestle.

Place the chickpeas in a food processor and process them to a pulp. Transfer to a large bowl and add the minced meat, onion, garlic, egg, Worcestershire sauce, tomato paste and parsley. Add the ground spices and season with salt and pepper. Mix together well.

Take small amounts of the mixture and shape into balls the size of cherry tomatoes. You should have about 60 balls. Place the spicy meatballs on a serving platter, and chill until ready to eat.

To make the harissa dip, stir together the yogurt, rose water and harissa and chill.

Heat the oil for deep-frying in a wok or deep pan to 375°F. If you do not have a cook's thermometer, test by dropping in a cube of day-old bread; it should brown in 30–60 seconds. Carefully transfer the wok or pan to a burner at the table.

Diners cook the meatballs for 3–5 minutes, then dunk them in the harissa dip.

INGREDIENTS

Serves 4–6

1 ounce cellophane noodles
9 ounces ground pork
1 bunch scallions, finely
    chopped
7 ounces bean sprouts
small bunch cilantro, chopped
1 tablespoon soy sauce
1 teaspoon Thai fish sauce
1 teaspoon brown sugar
9-ounce pack small spring
    roll wrappers (4^1/2 inches
    square)
1 tablespoon all-purpose
    flour mixed with
    1 tablespoon water
vegetable oil, for deep-frying
cilantro sprigs and lettuce
    leaves to serve

For the satay sauce
1 small fresh chile, seeded
1 garlic clove, finely chopped
1 tablespoon vegetable oil
14-fluid ounce can coconut milk
2 tablespoons brown sugar
4 tablespoons peanut butter
2 tablespoons chopped
    peanuts, to garnish

VARIATIONS

Ground chicken, chopped
shrimp and shredded
vegetables can also be used.

These delicious Vietnamese pork spring rolls, called *cha gio*, are often cooked fresh on stalls at the side of the road for passersby to snack on.

Spring Rolls
with Satay Sauce

Soak the cellophane noodles for 10 minutes in hot water to cover, then drain well and snip them into short lengths. Mix the noodles, pork, scallions and bean sprouts in a large bowl. Add the cilantro, soy sauce, fish sauce and sugar and combine.

Place a spring roll wrapper in front of you with a point facing you. Soften the wrapper by brushing with water. Place a teaspoonful of the filling just below the center, fold over to the nearest point and roll once. Fold in the sides to enclose, brush the edges with the flour and water, and roll up to seal. Repeat with the remaining wrappers.

Heat the oil for deep-frying in a wok or deep pan to 375°F. A cube of day-old bread should brown in 30–60 seconds. Carefully transfer the wok or pan to a burner at the table.

To make the satay sauce, pound the chile and garlic together in a mortar with a pestle. Heat the

oil in a frying pan and fry the chile paste for a few seconds, then add the coconut milk, sugar and peanut butter. Mix well and simmer for 5 minutes, then pour into a serving bowl and cool. Garnish with chopped peanuts.

Diners fry their spring rolls for 2–3 minutes, until golden brown. If you like, wrap each cooked roll in a lettuce leaf with cilantro. Serve with the satay sauce for dipping.

INGREDIENTS

Serves 4–6

7 ounces cod fillet,
  skin removed

7 ounces fresh white crab meat,
  or 2 x 4¹/4-ounce cans white
  crab meat, drained

1 tablespoon red curry paste

2 teaspoons Thai fish sauce

4 ounces green beans,
  finely chopped

7 ounces/3¹/2 cups fresh
  bread crumbs

vegetable oil, for deep-frying

For the relish

1 small cucumber

2 shallots, finely chopped

2 small red chiles, seeded and
  finely chopped

1¹/2 tablespoons
  superfine sugar

3 tablespoons rice vinegar

1 tablespoon water

COOK'S TIP

*When you are keeping oil
fondues hot at the table, it is
best to use a good quality
cook's thermometer, if you have
one, to keep a careful check on
the oil temperature.*

**These little crab cakes are firm and
meaty inside with a crispy coating and
distinctive flavors. They are served
with a red chile and cucumber relish.**

Crab Cakes
with Thai Cucumber Relish

Remove any remaining bones from the cod, then place in a food processor. Add the crab meat,
curry paste, Thai fish sauce and green beans, and pulse until blended. Chill for 1 hour.

With oiled hands, roll small quantities of the crab mixture into about 20 slightly flattened patties.
Roll them in the bread crumbs and place on a serving platter. Chill until ready to serve.

To make the cucumber relish, shred the cucumber on a mandolin or chop it finely. Transfer the
cucumber to a serving bowl and add the finely chopped shallots and chiles. Heat the sugar, vinegar
and water together in a small pan, stirring occasionally, until the sugar has dissolved, then allow to
cool. Pour the cooled liquid over the cucumber mixture, and place in serving saucers.

Heat the oil for deep-frying in a wok or deep pan to 375°F. If you do not have a cook's
thermometer, test by dropping
a cube of day-old bread into
the hot oil; it should brown
in 30–60 seconds. Carefully
transfer the wok or pan to a
burner at the table.

Each diner drops their own
crab cakes into the hot oil and
cooks them for 3–5 minutes,
or until they are golden
brown, and then removes
them with chopsticks, tongs or
little wire baskets.

Serve with the Thai
cucumber relish for dipping.

INGREDIENTS

Serves 4–6

1 medium eggplant

2 red bell peppers, seeded

9 ounces/2¼ cups all-purpose
flour, plus extra for dusting

4 baby squid, cut into rings

7 ounces green beans, trimmed

12 mint sprigs

oil, for deep-frying

2 egg yolks

16 fluid ounces/2 cups
iced water

1 teaspoon salt

gari (Japanese pickled ginger) or
grated ginger root, and grated
daikon or pink radishes,
to serve

For the dipping sauce

7 fluid ounces/scant
1 cup water

3 tablespoons mirin or
sweet sherry

¼ ounce bonito flakes

3 tablespoons soy sauce

VARIATIONS

• Any seafood is suitable for
cooking in a tempura batter.
Try mussels, clams, shrimp or
scallops, or slices of salmon,
cod, tuna or haddock.

• Cauliflower, broccoli, snow
peas and green beans work
well, too.

Crunchy battered vegetables and crisp squid rings are perfect with a piquant dipping sauce, daikon and pink, pickled ginger in this flavorful Japanese dish.

Tempura

To make the dipping sauce, mix the sauce ingredients together in a pan, bring to the boil and then strain into serving saucers and leave to cool.

Cut the eggplant and peppers into fine strips using a sharp knife or a mandolin. Put the flour for dusting into a plastic bag and add the squid. Shake the bag to coat the squid with a little flour, then place on a serving platter. Repeat with the vegetables and mint.

Heat the oil for deep-frying in a wok or deep pan to 375°F. If you do not have a cook's thermometer, test by dropping a cube of day-old bread into the hot oil; it should brown in 30–60 seconds. Carefully transfer to a burner at the table.

When ready to eat, beat the egg yolks and the iced water together. Tip in the flour and salt, and stir briefly. It is important that the tempura is lumpy and not mixed to a smooth batter.

Each diner dips the food into the batter and then immediately into the hot oil using chopsticks,

long forks or wire baskets. Fry for 2 minutes, or until crisp.

Serve the tempura dipped in the sauce, and accompanied by gari or ginger and daikon or radishes.

COOK'S TIP

If you cannot get hold of bonito flakes, an acceptable substitute would be to use 7 fluid ounces/ scant 1 cup well-flavored fish stock instead of the water to make the dipping sauce.

INGREDIENTS

Serves 4–6

4 corn on the cob
1 pound potatoes,
    peeled and cut into
    even-size pieces
2 eggs
dash of Tabasco sauce
1 teaspoon Worcestershire
    sauce
7 ounces/2 1/3 cups dry
    unsweetened shredded
    coconut
oil, for deep-frying
salt and ground black
    pepper
cilantro leaves, to serve

For the salsa

3 1/2 ounces peeled mango,
    finely diced
3 1/2 ounces peeled
    papaya, finely diced
1-inch piece ginger root,
    peeled and grated
1 shallot or 1/2 small red
    onion, finely chopped
rind and juice of 1 lime

A totally tropical, mellow but vibrant fondue that will perk up even the most tired of palates. Deep-fry coconut corn cakes and serve with piquant salsa.

Caribbean Corn Cakes with Tropical Salsa

Place the corn and potatoes in a large pan of boiling water and cook for 10–15 minutes, or until the potatoes are just tender. Drain.

Meanwhile, make the salsa by mixing all the ingredients in a bowl. Transfer the salsa to a serving bowl and leave to allow the flavors to blend.

Mash the potatoes and slice the corn kernels from the cobs. Put into a large bowl with the eggs and Tabasco and Worcestershire sauces.

Season with salt and pepper and mix well. Shape the mixture into about 18 small round pieces and flatten slightly. Place the coconut on a plate and press each cake into it so that it is coated with the coconut on all sides. Place on a serving platter and chill until ready to serve.

Heat the oil in a wok or deep pan to 375°F. If you do not have a cook's thermometer, test by dropping a cube of day-old bread into the hot oil; it should brown in 30–60 seconds. Carefully transfer to a burner at the table.

Invite the diners to carefully drop the corn cakes into the hot oil and leave them to cook for 3–5 minutes, or until they are golden brown. Fish the cakes out with wire baskets or tongs and eat topped with the salsa and cilantro leaves.

Sweet
fondues

These desserts are quite irresistible. Choose from creamy custard served with mini meringues, blackberry fondue with figs, luscious chocolate fondue or banana fritters with papaya cream.

INGREDIENTS

Serves 4–6

4 fluid ounces/½ cup milk

½ pint/1¼ cups light cream

1 vanilla bean, split lengthwise

1 fresh bay leaf

4 egg yolks

2 ounces/¼ cup vanilla-
    flavored superfine sugar

7 ounces/1¾ cups fresh
    summer berries,
    to serve

For the meringues

4 ounces/¾ cup fresh
    raspberries

3 egg whites

6 ounces/scant 1 cup
    superfine sugar

COOK'S TIPS

• For successful meringues, use
  a large bowl and make sure
  that both the bowl and whisk
  are scrupulously clean.

• Whisk the egg whites until
  they are very stiff before
  adding the sugar.

• When making the crème
  anglaise cook the eggs slowly
  and gently or they will curdle.
  Patience will be rewarded with
  a smooth, thickened custard.

Dainty meringues and fresh berries are dipped into a creamy egg custard, making this luscious fondue dessert a wonderful finale to a summer meal.

Crème Anglaise
with Raspberry Meringues

First make the meringues. Preheat the oven to 250°F/Gas ½ and line two baking trays with parchment paper. Place the raspberries in a food processor or blender and blend to a puree, then strain through a sieve. Whisk the egg whites until they hold stiff peaks. Add half the sugar, a tablespoonful at a time, whisking between each addition until you have a light, firm and glossy meringue. Fold in the remaining sugar.

Place small heaps of the meringue (about two teaspoonfuls) well apart on the baking trays, and make a slight hollow in the center of each with the back of a wet teaspoon. Place a teaspoonful of the raspberry puree into the hollow of each and then top with a little more meringue.

Bake the meringues for 1½ hours, or until crisp, yet still slightly soft in the center.

Heat the milk and cream in a pan with the vanilla bean and bay leaf until almost boiling. Whisk the egg yolks and sugar together in a large bowl until pale and creamy, then whisk in the hot milk and cream. Return to a low heat and stir constantly until thickened.

Transfer to a fondue pot on a burner at the table. Keep the crème anglaise warm over a very low heat, and serve it with the raspberry meringues and berries for dipping.

INGREDIENTS

Serves 4–6

7 ounces bittersweet chocolate

2 1/2 fluid ounces/ 1/3 cup strong
black coffee

3 ounces/scant 1/3 cup soft light
brown sugar

4 fluid ounces/ 1/2 cup
heavy cream

small, firm scoops of vanilla
ice cream decorated with
candied violets, to serve

For the poached pears

juice of 1 lemon

3 1/2 ounces/ 1/2 cup vanilla
superfine sugar

1–2 fresh rosemary sprigs

12–18 small pears, or 4–6
large pears

COOK'S TIPS

• *To make mini ice-cream balls,*
use a melon baller instead of
an ice-cream scoop. Dip the
melon baller in warm water
between scoops.

• *Ensure that the ice-cream*
balls are very firm before
serving: arrange them on a
metal tray as you scoop them
and then refreeze the balls for
at least an hour.

**Rosemary and vanilla-scented pears
and scoops of daintily decorated ice
cream are dipped into a rich chocolate
fondue for this splendid dessert.**

Bitter Chocolate Fondue with Poached Pears

To make the poached pears, put the lemon juice, sugar, rosemary sprigs and 1/2 pint/1 1/4 cups water in a pan large enough to accommodate the pears all in one layer. Bring to the boil, stirring occasionally, to ensure that the sugar dissolves in the water.

Peel the pears, and halve the large ones, if using, but leave the stalks intact. Add to the boiling syrup and spoon over to cover.

Cook for 5–10 minutes, depending on the size and ripeness of the pears, spooning the syrup over them and turning them frequently, until they are only just tender. Transfer the pears to a serving plate, then remove the rosemary sprigs from the syrup. Pull off about 1–2 tablespoons of the rosemary leaves and stir them into the syrup and then leave to cool.

Break the chocolate into pieces and place in a heatproof bowl over a pan of barely simmering water. Add the coffee and sugar and heat, without stirring, until the chocolate is melted. Stir in the cream and heat gently. Transfer the hot fondue to a fondue pot and place on a burner set at a low heat at the table.

Serve the pears and syrup together with the decorated vanilla ice cream to dip into the hot chocolate fondue.

INGREDIENTS

Serves 4–6

1 ³/4 pounds/7 cups
   blackberries
juice of 2 lemons
6 ounces/scant 1 cup
   superfine sugar
¹/2 pint/1 ¹/4 cups Zinfandel
   rosé wine
2 tablespoons cornstarch
   blended to a paste with
   about 2 tablespoons water
7 tablespoons crème de cassis
1 tablespoon chopped
   fresh mint
16 ripe, fresh figs, quartered

For the pastries

all-purpose flour and
   confectioners' sugar,
   for dusting and rolling
13 ounces puff pastry, thawed
   if frozen
10 ounces white marzipan
superfine sugar, for dusting

VARIATION

*Cubes of sweet breads such as
brioche or panettone would be
perfect with this fondue, as
would crunchy Italian cookies
such as cantucci or biscotti.*

**Spiral-shaped, crisp marzipan pastries
and sweet fresh figs are wonderful
dipped into a lemon-and-mint-scented
hot blackberry-and-wine fondue. Make
this in late summer or early autumn
when blackberries are plentiful.**

Blackberry Fondue with
Figs and Frangipane Pastries

To make the pastries, preheat the oven to 350°F/Gas 4, line a baking sheet with parchment paper, and dust a work surface with flour. Roll out the pastry to a 12 × 8-inch rectangle, then dust the work surface with confectioners' sugar and roll out the marzipan to the same size.

    Place the marzipan on top of the pastry, then roll both together to make a long sausage shape. Cut crosswise into ½-inch slices and arrange on the prepared baking sheet. Bake for 15 minutes, or until puffed and tinged golden brown. Transfer to a cooling rack, and dust with superfine sugar.

Blend the blackberries in a food processor with the lemon juice, then press through a sieve into a pan. Add the sugar and wine and bring to the boil, then simmer for 20 minutes, skimming off any scum that rises to the top. Stir in the blended cornstarch and cook, stirring, until thickened. Add the liqueur.

    Transfer to a fondue pot, add the mint, and place on a burner at the table. Serve with the pastries and figs.

INGREDIENTS

Serves 4–6

oil, for deep-frying

2 pounds bananas

juice of 1 lime

lime wedges and superfine
sugar, to serve

For the batter

6 fluid ounces/³/4 cup water

5 ounces/1¹/4 cups
all-purpose flour

4 ounces/1¹/3 cups
dry unsweetened
shredded coconut

¹/2 teaspoon salt

3 ounces/6 tablespoons
superfine sugar

1 egg, beaten

For the papaya cream

2 papayas, quartered, seeded
and skinned

juice of 1 lime

¹/2 pint/1¹/4 cups heavy cream

2 ounces/¹/2 cup confectioners'
sugar, sieved

Bananas, dipped in coconut batter, are fried at the table until soft inside and crisp outside. A lime-flavored papaya cream makes an exotic dip.

Banana Fritters with Papaya Cream

To make the batter, put all the batter ingredients in a bowl and mix together well using a wooden spoon. Leave to rest in a cool place for 20 minutes, then transfer the mixture to a serving bowl.

To make the papaya cream, put the papayas and the lime juice in a food processor or blender and process to a puree. Whip the cream until just beginning to thicken, then fold in the papaya purée and sugar. Spoon into serving dishes and chill.

Heat the oil for deep-frying in a wok or deep pan to 375°F. If you do not have a cook's thermometer, test by dropping a cube of day-old bread into the hot oil; it should brown in 30–60 seconds. Transfer the wok or pan to a burner at the table.

Peel the bananas, cut each in half lengthwise, and then cut each half crosswise into two slices about 3 inches long. Squeeze over the lime juice to prevent them discoloring, then transfer to a serving platter.

Each diner makes his or her own fritters by first dipping the banana slices in the batter to coat and then deep-frying them for about 30 seconds, or until golden and crispy. Drain the fritters on kitchen paper, squeeze over some lime juice and sprinkle with superfine sugar, then dip into the papaya cream and eat.

Index

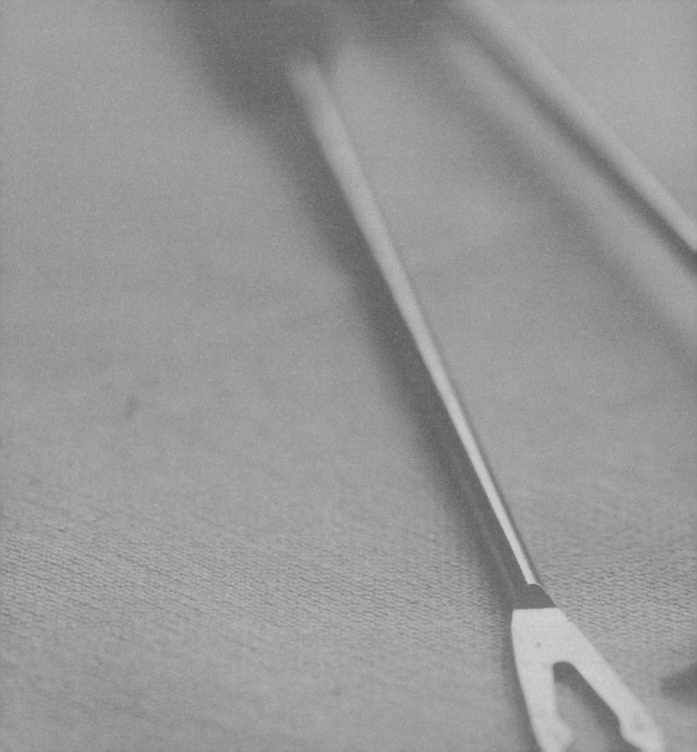